*Manifest $10,000*

"I have been following Cassie's work for a while and this one hits it out of the park. It explains not just the 'what,' but the 'why' of her manifesting system and how to use the system to put an extra 10,000 dollars in your life. I know where mine is going. Do you?"

— *Jeanne Andrus*

"I've read a lot of manifesting and LOA material. I've also read a lot about habit change, belief systems and the brains role in all this.

"Most manifesting books deal only with the mechanics of the law of attraction, they emphasize feeling good and often expect you to force yourself to completely reverse your thinking. That is where they fall down, because what you don't find out unless you dig into habits or how your brain works, is that it isn't so easy to do. It's also why most people put down the books and often the whole thought of manifesting anything.

"The big difference with this book is that it not only sets out ways to shift your relationship with money, it also highlights the places where you may fall down. It shows you the traps before you hit them, so that you can work out the best ways to negotiate your way past them and keep going. It helps you to not feel like a failure or that there is something wrong with you if you hit a snag. And that may be the biggest advantage of all.

"I've taken Cassie's course and I've read her other books. I consider myself a 'lazy manifestor' and by no means perfect at feeling good all the time, yet every time I read through Cassie's material, magic starts to happen and money starts to flow in.

"*Manifest $10,000* is an easy and enlightening read that starts another shift."

— *Kate Winch*

"Stand back and soak it all in – the universe loves you and gifts of money are on their way! This is a great read to take action and create the life you say you want but think you don't deserve or can't have. There are some great lessons inside on how we block ourselves unintentionally and even greater stories of those who have done great work and received abundance in many forms. In just days after reading this book, I manifested an extra $875 that was truly a gift from the universe. Get your copy today!"

— *Leslie Dougherty*

"This book brings the Law of Attraction (LOA) into focus. When I first learned of the LOA, I found much of the material to be filled with 'rainbows and magic.' However, the reality is that it can be difficult to continue using LOA techniques when the results are not immediate. Cassie Parks makes it easy to understand what is happening during the LOA process. She guides her students through the 'tough times' using her Manifest 10K course. This book thoroughly describes every instance of the process without added 'filler.' Cassie knows how to get to the point and relate to her readers. Her stories are amazing and relatable.

"I'm currently enrolled in Cassie's Manifest 10K course. This book simply makes too much sense. It's a great read, and especially helpful if one is considering enrolling in Cassie's course. Cassie has all of the angles covered when using the LOA, and reading this book will make you feel you can become a master of manifesting in 90 days."

*– Joseph DePasqua*

"I am a long time believer in Law of Attraction and really do believe we create what is in our lives... wanted and unwanted! I have mastered many areas of my life over the years and yet I am still not quite 'there' when it comes to business and finances. I feel very excited to realize that I have never really devoted much time to getting 'clear' on the future me, what my life would be like or even what I would be like if I was living the life I was wanting to create! I find it to be the missing link! :)

"The business strategies are excellent...explained well for beginners or those who need help with 'how to' as well as what not to do.

"I respond well to 'stories' – being a natural story teller myself, I so appreciated hearing some of Cassie's back stories and how we can learn and move forward.

"I'm looking forward to becoming more clear on my 'future me' and seeing the evidence of it playing out in my life!

Thanks Cassie!"

– *Katy Lowe*

# *Manifest* $10,000

*Learn How to Manifest 10,000
by Using the Law of Attraction and
Improving Your Money Mindset*

## CASSIE PARKS

NEW YORK

NASHVILLE  MELBOURNE

# Manifest $10,000

*Learn How to Manifest 10,000 by Using the Law of Attraction and Improving Your Money Mindset*

© 2017 Cassie Parks

Published in New York, New York, by Morgan James Publishing in partnership with Difference Press. Morgan James is a trademark of Morgan James, LLC. www.MorganJamesPublishing.com

The Morgan James Speakers Group can bring authors to your live event. For more information or to book an event visit The Morgan James Speakers Group at www.TheMorganJamesSpeakersGroup.com.

ISBN 978-1-68350-196-1 paperback
ISBN 978-1-68350-197-8 eBook
Library of Congress Control Number:
2016913955

**Cover Design by:**
Rachel Lopez
www.r2cdesign.com

**Interior Design by:**
Bonnie Bushman
The Whole Caboodle Graphic Design

**Editing:**
Grace Kerina

**Author's photo courtesy of:**
Aimee Starr

In an effort to support local communities, raise awareness and funds, Morgan James Publishing donates a percentage of all book sales for the life of each book to Habitat for Humanity Peninsula and Greater Williamsburg.

Get involved today! Visit
www.MorganJamesBuilds.com

# Table of Contents

## *Chapter 1*

# Introduction

*I* am guessing you discovered the Law of Attraction some time ago. You get it, you totally get it. When you realized you have the power to create your life the way you want it, that changed everything. Now you know that it is all possible.

In the beginning, you were so excited. You bought lots of books and you started studying. You started attacking your limiting beliefs – and things got better. In fact, they got a *lot* better, because you discovered the Law of Attraction (LOA) at the moment you needed it most. It was a less-than-ideal time in your life. Things were kind of crappy – okay, maybe they were really crappy. You were hurting and wanted to change. By a stroke of magic, exactly what you needed appeared. And you were so grateful. You dove in. And things got better.

That is probably the most common story of the way people get started with the Law of Attraction. Things in their life aren't going well, or they are hurting for some reason, or both, and they start looking for an answer, a way to change what is going on, a way to take hold of the steering wheel of their life. In that search, they stumble upon the magic and power of the Law of Attraction. Next, they start exploring the limiting beliefs they have and fixing those, one way or another, because they've figured out that if they have a limiting belief they won't get what they want. Honestly, when you first start uncovering and shifting limiting beliefs, it feels good. You feel a deep relief when you uncover and let those bad boys go.

After you let go of your limiting beliefs, you feel better and things start to flow. The better you feel, the more they start to flow. You start manifesting things, like free stuff and great parking spaces. You start nailing it and things start to feel even better. Life goes from crappy to pretty okay, and you travel along feeling good for a while.

Then you decide you want more. Parking spaces are awesome, but you want *more*, like a new car to park in that space. You aren't struggling to pay your bills, but you would really like to have the money to take that trip to the beach that is on your vision board. So, of course, you try to start upping your manifesting game, but for some reason it doesn't seem to be happening as easily as you thought it would. You try harder. You do more things. You start pulling books off the shelf and downloading new ones onto your iPad. In each book, you pick out the bits that you believe to be the missing pieces of your manifesting puzzle and put them on your manifesting "to-do" list. You do everything you think you're supposed to, but it's just not yielding the results you desire. You are not reading this book from the beach, after all.

"Why isn't it working?" you wonder. Then you come to the conclusion most of my clients come to – that there must be a limiting belief in your way. So you go back to trying to figure out your limiting beliefs, because if you could just figure those out you know you would get your manifesting back on track and be booking that plane ticket in no time. You do find some limiting beliefs, and you work on them. But you still don't get any closer to booking that plane ticket, and you don't feel the relief you felt when you first started shifting your limiting beliefs, so you assume there must *still* be a block of some kind, and you go looking for that. If you could just figure out what thoughts and beliefs are still blocking you, you would start manifesting the money and everything else you desire. When you don't start manifesting what you want, you keep digging for blocks and limiting beliefs.

*You are not alone.* Almost everybody goes through this, because doing what you're doing is how you got started. You're thinking to yourself, "I fixed my limiting beliefs and removed my blocks before and I started to manifest, so if I want to manifest more of what I desire, I should fix more of my limiting beliefs and remove my blocks." Of course that makes sense, because it's worked before.

I understand thinking that you have to fix all your limiting beliefs before you can move forward and create more of what you desire. Here's the thing, though – the Law of Attraction is that *like attracts like*. You *always* get more of what you focus on. When you start focusing on limiting beliefs, you will find them, and you will find more of them because that is what you are focusing on. The more you try to "fix" yourself, the more you will find that needs fixing. It's the way the system works.

My hunch is that when you shifted your focus to finding and fixing your limiting beliefs, things in your life started to deteriorate a little. Not a lot, and definitely not back to your pre-Law of Attraction days, but enough to notice. That is because you shifted your focus from "I've got this" to "Something is wrong," and that is going to have an impact on how your life flows. Where attention goes, energy flows.

Once you decide you are not as successful at manifesting as you would like to be and, therefore, "something is wrong," you start to try and counteract the problem by doing more and more things to try to manifest. Every day the list of things you think you *should* be doing to manifest gets longer, because you have started to do more research, bought a new book, and found a podcast. So, all that time, you are adding more and more manifesting tasks to your list.

Before you know it, your manifesting to-do list is longer than a grocery list for a whole month of meals. You start working harder and harder to try to manifest the things you want, but with little or no success. What does start happening is that you feel even more frustrated, overwhelmed, and bad about yourself because it seems like you will never get through the whole list. Every day it seems like the list grows, and you start doing fewer things on it and then you feel so bad, because you *know* this stuff is all important, and you *really* want to be living that life on your vision board, but you *just can't do it all*. And to top it off, it still does not seem to be working. You feel frustrated and overwhelmed and like you should be able to figure this out. You feel like you really should have figured it out (again) by now.

It's okay that you haven't.

You simply have not found the guide that takes you from Manifesting Level 101 to Expert Level. And you are definitely not alone in what you are feeling or doing.

Amanda, one of my clients, sums up this feeling: "I was getting down on myself and being a little frustrated. I really felt like nothing was working or even like I wasn't doing anything right." The majority of my clients feel this way when they first come to me. They have been adding to their manifesting to-do lists and doing more and learning more and not feeling like it's working. They grow even more frustrated – and have even come close to giving up a couple of times. Amanda felt that way as well. She admitted that she once threw her notebook across the room and said, "This isn't for me."

I invite you to follow me through the next pages to learn the process Amanda learned, which, in her words, "was really when the magic started happening and I really understood a lot better how all this works." You will learn how you can "level up" your manifesting game to manifest $10,000 in 90 days, which will build a foundation and give you practice and experience so you can continue upleveling your manifesting game and create all the "big" stuff you desire.

Honestly, I do not know how this $10,000 will show up in your life. It could come a little at a time or in one big check for $10,000 that you were not expecting. When I polled participants who took my course and learned what I am about to teach you, 100% of them said that the money did not show up the way they expected. Later in the book, I'll tell you why I picked $10,000 as the amount.

*Chapter 2*

# How People Think Money Manifests

Here are some common, but ineffective, ways people generally "think" surprise money manifests: winning the lottery, inheriting a bunch of money, magically finding out there's money for them on an "unclaimed money" list, or creating an in-depth plan and following it with great intention.

Let's talk about the lottery first. I see this intention a lot. People want to win the lottery because they think it's the only way to get the big money they desire into their lives. Can you use the Law of Attraction to win the lottery? Absolutely! You can find stories online about how people have done it.

People "try" to win the lottery all the time, because they think it's the only way to get what they desire. So they start visualizing winning and they start making sure they play all the time. And they start repeating affirmations like, "I am a lottery winner." They take the Jackpot picture and put it on their vision board. They do the whole list of things that they think is going to make them win the lottery.

The problem is with believing that the lottery is the only way to get the money, because that doesn't leave room for the Universe to do its magic. By turning all your attention and beliefs to winning the lottery, you put in a very specific order to the Universe and focus all your attention on that.

The truth is that very few people actually want to win the lottery. What they *really* want is the money that comes from winning the lottery. Because they think "winning the lottery" is the only way to get the money they want, they turn their manifesting energy toward *winning* and thus away from what they really want, which is *the money*.

Another common way people think money manifests is by someone dying and leaving an inheritance. Sometimes it does happen this way. However, no one wants anyone they love to have to die in order for them to get an inheritance. I totally understand that.

Here's where your brain can get in the way. If the only way it can come up with to manifest more money is for someone to die, and you don't want that, you are going to unconsciously resist manifesting money – because you don't want someone to die. That totally makes sense, but it can throw a big kink in your manifesting that you might not even know is there.

A third common way people think big money is going to manifest in their lives is through money that's out there already with their name on it, but that they don't know about and, therefore, is unclaimed. You have probably seen the commercials where they say to go check such-and-such government website to see if you have unclaimed money that needs to be collected by you.

If you believe that is the only way more money can manifest, you start checking that website religiously. It turns into an obsession, because you are sure that if you keep doing your manifesting list then your name is going to show up on that list. This obsession not only limits your opportunity to manifest, it creates a vibration that repels money. You are constantly "looking for" money, which means you don't believe you already have it. This is like saying to yourself over and over again that there is no money for you. Do you want to attract more of that?

A fourth way people think they are going to manifest money is by devising a plan and going to work on that plan. For example, one of my clients, Lynn, wanted to make a million dollars a year. She came up with a bunch of figures to make that happen. My head was spinning by the time she got done presenting them. It was a solid plan, but I could feel that it was uninspired. It only took a few minutes of talking for her to see that she was trying to *control* the way the money was going to manifest, instead of *allowing* a path to more money to reveal itself.

This happens all the time. You decide you want to manifest money, so you set one intention, and then you go to work planning and executing. This way can work. However, it's not actually using the Law of Attraction. It's about brute force and hard work. I have found that to be the long, slow, hard path. This method is especially common among business owners, because the only way they see that more money can come in is if they work harder.

If you think any of the methods above are the only ways money can manifest into your life, you are significantly limited. There are an *infinite* number of ways money can flow into your life – if you allow it. The natural thing, when you're still working toward LOA mastery, is to think that you have to figure out how it's going to happen. You don't.

When you've really leveraged the power of the Law of Attraction, you know that your job is to *become* the person who has the money, and allow the Universe to do the heavy lifting. One of the ways to open yourself up to how many possibilities there are for manifesting money by allowing the Universe to work its magic, is to read or hear stories about how money manifested for other people.

## Chapter 3

# Stories About How Money Manifests

*I* told you about how people often think money manifesting happens. Now I'd like to share with you how it actually happens. When I asked successful money manifestors who had taken my course if money manifested the way they thought it would, all of them said no – how it happened was a surprise.

I have found that money manifestation tends to happen in three main ways. I'll share stories about each of these categories, for a couple of reasons. Primarily, I want to show you how money actually manifests, but, also, reading these stories is going to amp up your belief about what is possible and open up your brain to seeing more and more possibilities, which is going to lead to more money manifesting.

Always Possible but Highly Unlikely

When I tell someone about my program, Manifest 10K (www.manifest10k.com), and they are a business owner, I often get the question, "Well, if someone is an employee, how is it possible to manifest money?" There are many ways, but magical promotions and raises are a few.

First, let's talk about Christine. She was focused on manifesting her $10,000 when, out of the blue, she received a promotion. Here is Christine's story in her words: "I have news. I received an unexpected promotion at my corporate job. They created a position for me and I am receiving a promotion to fill it. I haven't received the exact salary amount, but it is about $8K more (about $5K more after taxes) annually, and my bonus percentage eligibility is increasing from 15% to 25%. So, overall, if the company makes its numbers for the year, in March I will be eligible to receive a gross bonus of about $11 to $22K – more than I am eligible for now. This is so cool, and it starts with my next pay period!"

Christine was focused on manifesting $10,000, but she manifested so much more. She definitely didn't expect for it to manifest as a promotion. The company made up a new position for her, so that was something she could not have foreseen occurring.

I had a similar experience when I was working my corporate job. I set the intention to get a 20% raise. I had done that the year before, without even knowing how raises were given in the company, and manifested a 20% raise. I decided I wanted to do it again the next year, so I set the intention for a $9,000 raise. When the time of year came for raises, I got a $3,000 raise, which was good, but wasn't the 20% I'd intended. Rather than get upset or feel like I failed, I celebrated and let it go. About five months later, out of the blue, I was offered a promotion that came with another $7,000 increase in my salary. It was a position created to support the corporation's growth. At first, my boss had not considered me for the job, because it was a higher level position than I was technically qualified for, but then someone above my boss in the company suggested that she see if I was interested before they looked for an outside hire. It might have taken a few extra months, but I manifested the 10K, just like Christine did, even though neither of us knew in advance exactly how it would happen.

Nan lost her job in the middle of taking the Manifest 10K course. She emailed me to ask for help and I told her to keep doing the exercises so she would stay focused on manifesting and not lack. She did, and received an unexpected payout from her former employer that was $10,000. A few months later, she received a job offer for more money than she'd been earning in her old job. The new job also gave her a better work/life balance than her former job. She not only manifested more money, but more time, as well.

When I asked Nan if her manifestation happened the way she'd thought it would, she said, "No. I was hoping for a big check to just show up. It sort of did, but in a different way."

In the same vein, Joy, another of the Manifest 10k participants, manifested her $10,000 in 90 days from additional sales commissions at her job. That was on top of what she normally made in 90 days.

Being in alignment with money makes it easier for money to flow into your life. Are you feeling the possibilities opening up as you read these stories?

One of the participants in Manifest 10k, Jen, manifested $100,000 on long-shot investments that came through while she was taking the course. It was so crazy and seemed so ridiculous to her, yet she said she realized it was the power of focus that made it happen. She also manifested more than $9,000 in addition to the $100,000 during her 90 days in the program.

I love this story from my client, Sasha, about how she manifested over $10,000 by looking at money through a different lens. The money she manifested had always been there, she just hadn't seen it because she'd had a "lack" mindset instead of an activated "abundance" mindset. Here's what she said: "When I started working with Cassie I felt a jolt of courage to start doing detective work on my money – where I was overpaying for things, account activity, etc. What I discovered was stunning. I found that my cell bill had escalated when I'd changed some devices, and finding that out allowed me to ask my sister to adjust how much she was paying in (we shared a cell phone account). She wrote me a check covering her bill for the new rate through the end of the year. I also found an IRA that I'd thought had lost its value. On the contrary, it had quadrupled its value! I also changed an underperforming account to a fund with better rates. I was able to see the wisdom I had been missing and I applied to other accounts, adding to my good feelings." Sasha manifested more than $10,000 in 90 days. She said, "The Manifest 10K process changed my belief that I was a money hot mess to the belief that I am someone who actually has good instincts and can courageously act on my own behalf."

When *you* change, everything changes. In Sasha's case, what changed was the way she saw herself in terms of money – and that changed everything about money. So often, it's not that there is a lack of money, it's that you *think* there is a lack of money, and that affects your experience. Shifting your focus to allowing money lets you see what you did not see while your mind was focused on the lack in your life.

It is definitely possible that when you have work done on your house, the contractor could lower the bill, although I had never heard of that happening – until Josh participated in Manifest 10K. Here's his story which took place right after his kitchen remodel was completed: "I was originally quoted an estimate of around $20,000. When the contractor met with me after the job was done, he handed me the final bill and I noticed it wasn't itemized. He told me that was because I was easy to work with and went along with his suggested changes. Even though the changes increased my cost, he didn't want to charge me for them. He even fixed some unexpected termite damage he found after digging up the old floor and removing my old dishwasher. I paid a total of $14,200, which made my manifestation $4,800."

When your money vibe is activated, like Josh's was during his remodel, the possibilities of how money will flow into your life are infinite.

Just like it is always possible someone will charge you less than they quoted, it is also possible that your family could give you money. During the Manifest 10K course, Nicole manifested lots of money. At one point in the program, she and her fiancé were having such tight finances that they were running out of money for food. In addition, they had a wedding to finish paying for. Nicole's estranged family came together to help her out by paying $6,000 for the wedding. That might not seem like manifesting, but her family had never given her a dime before. Nicole also started getting proposals for freelance work at rates that were nearly three times what she was making at her job at the time.

When you change, your experiences change.

Molly had just gotten a job at a boutique, after being unemployed for a month and a half. The boutique job was only for 12 hours a week. Due to a difficult time in her past, Molly had "a ton of debt – the type that you figure you will be paying off until you die." Her daughter was getting ready to go to college, so the burden of the debt was causing deep stress in Molly's life. That is when we connected online, and she decided she was meant to join my course.

While participating in the course Molly got a message from someone in her life that said, "I put twenty-five in your account." Molly assumed that was twenty-five dollars and was excited because it would help her make it through until payday. The next day, when she opened her bank account, she saw an extra $25,000 in there. She was sure someone had made a mistake when they'd entered the deposit information, and that it would go away. It didn't. The person in her life had *meant* to put the $25,000 into her account. She immediately went online and paid off all of her credit cards. In a matter of a half hour, her entire financial life changed. Later that afternoon, she found a dime, and her boss gave her a $50 gift card.

Appreciating yourself and all the money that comes into your life, like even a dime, can change your financial situation instantly. Molly's story is similar to Nicole's in that neither of them had been given money before. How we show up in the world matters. When you step into abundance and money flow, the world responds, often in the most unlikely ways.

The thing everyone wants when it comes to money is for it to come easily. Jill Angie, founder of Not Your Average Runner (notyouraveragerunner.com), had been trying to make her life easier by finding a new t-shirt supplier. She was not successful and had given up by the time she started the Manifest 10K process. Within a few days of following the process, she was contacted by someone offering to do exactly what she wanted with her t-shirts, which was to make her life easier, and doubling the amount of money she was making from each shirt. That shift to a new supplier will lead to more than $10,000, and now Jill has more free time to enjoy the money she's making.

Most people want money to come easier. They don't want to have to work so hard for it. As Jill's story shows, that's possible.

**Totally Magical**

Another way money manifests is by total magic you couldn't have imagined. One of my personal favorite stories is about a refund I got for a house I purchased. When I bought the house, I offered a price, but the owners declined it because they were a non-profit. So I purchased the house for the price they wanted. Two years later, I was working my money manifesting skills and I received a call. A woman explained who she was and asked if I remembered that I'd bought my house from their company. She then said, "This is going to sound really weird, but we owe some money back." The funny thing is, they sent me almost $2,000 back, and when I was buying the house they wouldn't sell it to me for $1,000 less. That was manifesting magic.

**Winning**

Some of the money that manifests in the Manifest 10K course *does* come from lottery-type winnings.

Many participants win some money from the casino or the lottery if they play. In fact, Aaron manifested $10,000 in 90 days at the casino. He kept amping his money vibe and trusting his intuition, and he kept winning.

I love Aaron's story, and I really enjoyed watching him go through the process of manifesting. However, his story is the least typical way money manifests with the Manifest 10K process. He will even say he's not a heavy gambler. He considers gambling more of a way to "practice letting go" than a way to manifest money.

Winning the money is always an option, but it's good to know that there are other ways money shows up, too. In Aaron's case, he was not attached to *how* the money showed up. He was not *trying* to win. He just focused on his money mindset and followed his intuition. The way money flowed to him just happened to be through the casino.

The more you raise your money mindset, the more your intuition will speak to you and direct you toward money. It is possible it could lead you to the casino, but even more possible that it will lead you to something you did not expect or see as an option before.

## Combination

When the goal is to manifest $10,000, it often happens through a combination of all of the above. Laura manifested more than $10,000 in 90 days through a combination of each of these ways. In fact, most participants in the Manifest 10K program experience successful manifestations in all areas. Another participant, Julie, manifested over $20,000 in 90 days – also through a combination of all of these ways.

## Chapter 4

# Why People Don't Manifest Money Quickly and Easily

*Y*ou just read some stories about how money has manifested quickly and easily into people's lives. Why doesn't everyone manifest money quickly and easily? In the Introduction, I said that most people find the Law of Attraction when something is wrong, so they work on their limiting beliefs and feeling better. Then they get good at manifesting free stuff and parking spots. What comes next is manifesting the "big stuff," like $10,000. Making the transition from free stuff to big money sends most people back to a mindset of trying to fix things.

These are the reasons people have for not manifesting money: you force it, your brain gets in the way, you have limiting beliefs, you're working the list, you're doing more, you're not being clear about what's wanted, your lack of focus, your beliefs about debt, and/or not noticing the evidence.

## You Force It

One of the reasons you have gotten twisted up trying to manifest money is because your brain can only think of so many ways it can manifest before one of two things happens. Either you go fully into trying to manifest by using the ways you think are possible, or you put together a list of manifesting techniques from a bunch of different sources and start doing all of them.

In the first case, deciding to manifest based on a way you think it will happen, you go to work trying to make that happen. That is actually using brute force but calling it the Law of Attraction. One of the clues you are going about it this way is that you devise a plan.

Very often, if you set an intention to manifest a bunch of money – let's use $10,000 – and then, ten minutes later, come up with a plan to execute manifesting your intention, you are controlling the how instead of allowing your intention to do the manifesting. Why is this? Because in the ten minutes between setting an intention and devising a plan, it's unlikely that you have become a person who has an additional $10,000. If you intend to have something that you don't yet have, your job is not to create a plan to get it, but rather to become the person who has it. When you step into the *beingness* of a person who has $10,000 – rather than the *doingness* of the person with the specific plan – the money either just shows up, or you are led down an easy path to creating it.

## Your Brain Resists the Change

In the second case, where you put together a list of manifesting techniques from a bunch of different places, your brain starts resisting because it can't come up with a plan of how to make it all happen. Your brain's primary job is to keep you safe. Most people don't consider money dangerous, and likely neither does your brain. However, your brain likes to know where you are going so it can make sure it and you are safe. Most manifesting programs don't take this part into account. They don't warn you that, at some point, your brain may take over and try to steer you back, or try to alert you to the fact that, as you step into the version of yourself who has $10,000, you might experience brain detox, which is the process your brain sometimes goes through when you are shifting your focus and how you feel about money. When you experience brain detox or resistance, it can be hard to continue doing the full list of manifesting techniques and it's easy to get frustrated, because your emotions feel out of whack and you feel worse than normal so it feels like it's not working. This is the point where many people stop, which actually causes you to lose momentum and does not allow the shift to take place.

Brain interference is one of the main reasons I see for why people get off the manifesting train too early and thus do not experience success. How do you fix this? First, just the awareness of the fact that it happens will help. The other thing that helps immensely is following a proven LOA system.

Most people, when they get off track, will simply go back to "the list" and start doing every manifesting technique under the sun. The reason this isn't hugely successful is because it's about taking bits and pieces from a whole bunch of different LOA systems. That's like trying to bake a cake by using bits of ingredients from recipes for making brownies, cookies, and a cake. Each recipe turns out fine when it's followed just on its own, but swapping out and mixing up the recipes probably isn't going to yield a yummy cake. It *might* turn out well – or you might end up wasting a whole bunch of time and energy because what you created isn't edible. Similarly, when you put pieces together from a whole bunch of manifesting systems, it's possible that it could work, but it's also possible that you'll waste a bunch of time and energy and not get the results you were intending. Following a system that has a structure in place for keeping you on track in those moments when your brain wants you to get off track is super helpful.

## Limiting Beliefs

As I said in the Introduction, people will often go backward in the process of manifesting money. When they decide to manifest more money and it doesn't happen right away, they start looking for a limiting belief they can "fix" so they can start manifesting more money. And then... you know what happens – they find more limiting beliefs that need fixing. And, thus, the cycle continues, because the more you look for limiting beliefs and work on fixing them, the more you become someone who has something wrong with them that prevents them from manifesting money.

Every time you take the stance that "there must be a limiting belief in the way," you are both telling the Universe there is a reason what you want can't happen and reinforcing the belief in your brain that when it's not working it's because there's something wrong with you and, therefore, you aren't a person who can manifest more money into their life. Eventually, whether you're aware of it or not, you start believing that you aren't a person who can manifest money until you are "fixed."

Have you done that before? I did it – many, many times. And it never helped more money come into my life. In fact, it repelled money. I couldn't figure out why I was repelling money when I was trying so hard to fix everything about myself, but I felt like I was going backward with money. This is exactly why: I was trying to "fix" my way into manifesting. As long as you are being a version of yourself that needs fixing, you cannot also be a version of you who is manifesting money quickly and easily. Those are two different people and, while they have similarities, because they are both you, the differences will keep the money at bay.

You don't have to fix yourself in order to manifest more money. You simply have to step into the version of yourself that is *experiencing* the money you wish to have. It might sound complicated right now, but, trust me, it is easier than trying to fix yourself. I'll walk you through the process later in the book. Right now, take a deep breath and say – out loud or to yourself – "I am good enough right now to manifest more money into my life." How did that feel? Are you able to breathe deeper? Do you feel lighter? More free? These better feelings are going to do more for you in terms of manifesting money than fixing any belief will.

**Working the List**

Another reason people don't manifest money is that they're doing a whole bunch of things on their list of ways to manifest things, and they're trying to *make things work*. What I have found when I ask clients about their "lists" is that it's a bunch of random stuff they've picked up from a lot of different sources. All of the things on the list probably work perfectly well. However, when you start "doing your list" instead of increasing your focus on what you desire, it divides your focus and makes what you're doing less effective. The more you add to the list, the more you send out a signal that it's not working, so you have to do more. That is hard work. When "doing" and "hard work" are your focus, what are you going to get more of?

You cannot create what you want in the energy of what you do not want. What that means is, if you want money because it is going to make your life easier, you cannot work *harder* to manifest it. You have to somehow work easier. You have to find your way to a place that mirrors what your desire is going to *feel* like. If having more money would make your life easier, you have to be in a place of ease now, even before the money manifests. Adding more and more to your to-do list for manifesting is the opposite of creating ease. It also is likely creating a whole bunch of negative feelings – like possibly guilt, shame, overwhelm, or frustration. Those feelings will repel money.

Look over your list and evaluate why you are doing what. Are you doing the things on your list because they make you feel more like someone who has the money you desire? In other words, are they things that are actually helping you step into the *beingness* of someone who has money? Or are they things you're doing in the hope that they will work to manifest money? The most important things to do are the things that tap you into the *feeling* of abundance and that help you *be* the version of yourself that has money.

The good news here is that you don't have to do anything to "try to manifest." When you learn to prune your list down based on what helps you step into *being* someone with money, the list will get a lot smaller and a lot easier to do. Your list will then be more powerful and more effective.

**Doing More**

This reason is very closely related to the one above. The ultimate goal of the "list" should be to move you into the *beingness* of the version of yourself who has what you desire. So often people think if they *do* more, they will *get* more. I have seen it proven time and time again that if you do *less* with intention you will create *more*. You can breathe a huge sigh of relief right now, because you aren't going to put this book down and need to add ten more things to your "list." How does it feel to know you can do less and manifest more?

The goal with every single manifesting tool that you are using should be to bring you closer in sync with the version of yourself that has what you desire and is living their life accordingly. You have probably heard this a thousand times, but I'm going to say it again: you have to *be* the person who already has what you desire.

What does that really mean? It means you can't do ten money manifesting exercises and go to the store with a head full of the thought that you don't have enough money to make the choices you want to make at the store. It means choosing to appreciate what is in front of you, rather than lamenting about what you don't have. It's not the hour you spend on your manifesting practices that matters the most. It's who you are *being* the other 23 hours. Yes, what you *do* matters, but it gets erased if you walk around all day *being* a person who does not have money.

Maybe that last line totally makes sense and yet you are wondering, "But how?" The how takes practice and being diligent, but it is definitely possible, and we're going to discuss it in the next chapter.

**Not Being Clear About What's Wanted**

The next reason people don't manifest money is because they're not clear about what they actually want. People think they want to manifest money. If that was true and I walked up and handed you a dollar, would you consider your manifestation a success? You may say, "Oh! No, I meant I wanted $10,000." So often, people just ask for "money." That is too broad. That could literally mean any amount of money – from a penny to an infinite number of dollars.

That is why this book is called *Manifest $10,000* instead of *Manifest Money*. The book's intention was clear when you picked it up: you're going to learn how to manifest a specific amount of money.

Now let's go a step further in clarity. Truthfully, it's not even the $10,000 that you really want; it's what you want to get with your $10,000. I'm guessing that what you want the money for is something like this: $3,000 for that beach vacation, $2,000 to pay off your car, $1,000 to go shopping, $1,000 to give away, and $3,000 to put in savings. Even if I don't have it quite right, you're probably thinking and calculating your own list in your head right now, which is awesome. That means you're getting more clear about what you desire.

Visualizing *that* list is probably a lot more fun than just imagining $10,000 dollars in your hands or your bank account. It's fun to imagine yourself on the beach, or driving your car knowing that you own it free and clear. What song is playing the first time you drive after your car is paid off? Or you feel yourself writing a check to your favorite charity and knowing what a difference it's going to make to them.

Now get even clearer and define what you're going to do with the money you no longer have to pay toward the car, now that your car is paid off. What will you do with that $300? Add in a weekly massage? Go out to a fancy dinner a couple of times a month? Have a weekend getaway? What is doing those things going to feel like?

Can you see how important clarity is? It drives everything else. When you start out crystal clear, it makes everything you do in terms of manifesting greater. There's a bonus that comes along with being super clear, and that is the Universe knowing what you *actually* want, which makes it much easier to deliver. For example, if your beach vacation were to manifest differently than you manifesting the money first and then using it to pay for the beach vacation you want, would that be just as good? There are so many examples of people in the Manifest 10K course who get exactly what they wanted the $10,000 for, but who get it directly, without manifesting the money. The money really is the middle man, and the Universe can often cut it out altogether when you're clear about what you really desire.

## Lack of Focus

Being clear can help you avoid the next reason people don't manifest money quickly and easily, which is that they are focused on the wrong thing. What you focus on matters, especially when it comes to manifesting money. The biggest mistake I see people make is that they're trying to manifest being out of debt. What you focus on grows, so if you focus on getting out of debt you're likely to create... more debt. Even if you do get out of debt, the likelihood that something will happen that puts you right back in is high, because that is where your focus has been, so you are going to get more of it. This is the way the Law of Attraction works. The Universe doesn't say, "Oh, I'm pretty sure debt isn't what they want, so let's give them something else instead." The Universe just gives you more of what you focus on.

I had to learn this lesson myself. When I was focused on getting out of debt, it seemed like every month I was somehow adding to my debt. I wouldn't mean to, but I would forget my debit card, so I'd put something on my credit card and then forget to pay off the new charge when I got home. Then I would do it again and, at the end of the month, my debt would have gone higher. That kept happening until I realized I was focusing on what I didn't want more of. I started to focus on what I did want: money for taking vacations and getting massages.

This reason trips people up because, like I did, they think they *are* focusing on what they want – getting out of debt – but it's not *actually* what they want. If you want to get out of debt, what you likely want is the extra money that will give you each month, or the freedom you'll feel knowing the debt has been taken care of. You don't want to be "out of debt," you want something beyond that. You want what being out of debt will get you. If you don't figure out what *that* is, and start focusing on it, it will be hard to manifest the money to get out of debt.

I recently talked to a man who told me he could visualize paying off his mortgage, but there didn't seem to be any depth to that intention. He wanted advice on how to visualize it better. I explained this concept about focusing on debt and asked him why he wanted to pay his mortgage off. I suggested he start thinking about what his life would look like a year after he paid off his mortgage, because it's the life beyond the mortgage that he really wanted to manifest. He thought about it and realized that what he really wanted was the option to not have to go to work if he chose not to. What he really wanted to manifest was *freedom*. Do you see that freedom is a completely different focus point than debt?

When you master the ability to define and focus on what you really want, manifesting becomes easy. You get to a point where all you have to do is make a decision and laser focus on what you actually desire and it will show up quickly and easily.

**Beliefs About Debt**

Speaking of debt, another debt-related reason people don't manifest money is because they hold the belief that it is the debt that's holding them back, so they want to figure out how to get it out of the way so they can move forward. But, again, as long as they're focused on debt, they're going to create more of it. People often think that debt is what's holding them back. It's not. It's the obsession with it and the attachment to it as being negative that holds them back.

People try to shift their feelings to be positive about debt. That is a big shift and can take a lot of effort, but it's still not a focus on what is actually wanted. The answer is to find a way to see debt as neutral. It is what it is. It's already there and it can either continue to consume your focus, which will create more of it, or you can leave it alone and instead shift all that energy onto focusing on what you do want more of – the beach, vacation, freedom, whatever it is.

I used to obsess over how much debt I had before I understood this manifesting block. When I understood it, I set up automatic payments to pay off the debt, and left the debt alone. Instead of focusing on the debt, I put all of my energy into what I did want. Soon, because there was no energy left for the debt, it shrank to nothing. I kid you not, I do not even remember paying off my last couple of credit cards because I had done such a good job of focusing on what I wanted that there was no energy left for even the end of the debt.

Here is the reality of debt: in the beginning, while you're learning to manifest money, it's easier to manifest a monthly payment than it is to manifest the amount that would pay off the debt in full. That's because of where your focus is. If you can manifest the money for what you desire, does it really matter if you have debt?

**Not Noticing the Evidence**

The last thing I see that keeps people from manifesting money is that they don't notice the evidence that their money vibe is shifting. They get stuck on looking for that big number – $10,000 – to show up, so they miss all the little amounts that are adding up to $10,000 and the magic happening around them that is momentum in the direction they desire. When you pay attention and put energy and focus onto what is going right, things go right more often. You get more of what you want quicker and easier. This requires you to start noticing all the little things that mean money is on the way.

———————

In order to manifest more money into your life it takes shifting all the issues I've discussed in this chapter. There is an order in which to focus on things that makes it happen faster and more easily, which I'll tell you about in the next chapter.

## Chapter 5

# How to Manifest $10,000

*I*n Chapter 4 we talked about why people don't manifest money when they're using the Law of Attraction. They're often doing all the things they've heard to do, and even things that I would say to do, but it's not working because they're not going deep enough. If they're doing things out of order, that can have a big impact on the amount of success they experience.

The following process creates a vacuum for money attraction. In addition, it gets your brain on board with the process so that it's working *with* you instead of *against* you. The process is comprised of eight phases that build on each other to create momentum and success. The entire process is filled with belief-amping, which is pivotal for easing resistance and opening up your brain to see more and more possibilities.

### 1. Get Clear About What You Want

Earlier, I pointed out how important clarity is because, if you're not clear, it's possible to focus your energy on something you don't actually want, and you'll create more of it. It's important to drill down until you get to absolute clarity.

The first question to ask to get clear about what you're manifesting is, "What am I going to do with the $10,000 I manifest?" Write down a list. Get really clear about every dollar of the $10,000 and what you're going to do with it. For example, I've been using $3,000 as the number you might want to manifest for your beach vacation. Is that number correct? Look up where you would want to go and get all the costs for airline tickets, hotel, food, spending money. Are you treating your best friend to the trip as well? Get as accurate as possible when making your list. Why is this important? It goes back to *being*.

Look at it this way: if you had the $10,000 in your hands right now, you would be doing the research to see exactly how much the plane ticket is going to be, and looking up and comparing hotels or other places to stay. You would have some idea of what amount you would like to have for spending money and adventures while you're there. Have you ever planned a trip where you just assumed it would be $3,000 even? Probably not, because that just isn't how it's done. When you invest the time and energy in researching the details, you're *being* the person who's going on that trip. If you just throw out a guess of a number to do this assignment, you're *being* someone who's not actually going on a trip. Your behavior determines your *beingness*, and your *beingness* determines your manifesting success.

Go through the process of getting clear details about everything you desire to use your $10,000 for – and don't stop until you have allocated the entire $10,000.

If part of your list includes paying off a debt, get the actual payoff number. Because of interest, that can be different than the number on your last statement. If you were going to actually pay off the debt, you would know the number. After you figure out what the payoff amount is, determine what you will use the additional money for each month, now that you're not paying it to service that debt.

Time and again, people manifest what's on the list whether they get the money first or just directly get what they wanted the money for. Personally, I manifested a free place to stay on a vacation, and I manifested a couch the last time I went through this process. Part of my list of what I was going to use the $10,000 for was for a place to stay during a vacation to San Diego. Then I was offered an almost-free place. I also clarified that I intended to buy a couch with part of my $10,000. Then I was given the perfect couch – it was purple and perfect for my space. There are so many ways for what you desire to be delivered.

Can you see how getting really clear increases your resonance with the $10,000? Can you also see how it opens the door for the Universe to work more of its magic?

When you start manifesting, it's common to just put out there what you want to manifest, and that works well in the beginning, but as your desire grows to manifest bigger things, like more money, clarity becomes more important.

I have tested this and found that better results come when an intention is set to manifest a specific amount, as opposed to just "money." When I first created the Manifest 10K program, I called it Money, Money, Money. There was no focus point in terms of dollar amounts. The first assignment I gave to people in the program was to get clear about what they were manifesting the money for. When I started asking participants to add it up and see what the number was, to put a number value to what they wanted, they became more successful at manifesting, because then it wasn't only about "more money," it was about a specific amount of money and also about what the money was wanted for, and their brains could get on board much easier. Their desires became tangible. Manifesting became easier because they didn't feel overwhelmed by thinking they needed to create a mass of money in general, but could focus on a specific amount. Most of the time, the amount they were intending, when they added it up, was much less than they'd thought it would be.

Start by focusing on an amount that would drastically improve your life. Many people feel like their life can't change in a big way until they manifest millions of dollars, but that isn't true. Just look at how different your life is going to be when you manifest your $10,000.

As I took people through the process of finding the amount that would change their life, the average was about $10,000, which is one of the reasons I changed the course title to Manifest 10K. 10K is a big enough number that it's a stretch, and so you have to learn to let go of the how, but it's also not so big that it's overwhelming and feels like it will never happen.

This is the perfect way to start playing with manifesting money. Once you feel good about the process, you can open up and manifest more and more. Also, when you have enough, it's much easier to manifest more than enough. People try and go from feeling like there is "not enough" to "more than enough" right away, but finding your way to "enough" will lead to much greater success than going straight for "more than enough." If we think of it like dating, "more than enough" is like marriage. Some people can jump straight from the first date into marriage and make it last, but the majority can't. "Not enough" is like being single. How about starting to date, then moving to the boyfriend/girlfriend stage, which is like "enough," and then moving onto marriage, which is like "more than enough"?

Nan, who was introduced in one of the money manifesting stories in Chapter 3, decided during her first time through the Manifest 10K course that she was going to go for $100,000 instead of just $10,000, even though when she told me that I advised against it for the reasons I gave above. It didn't work. It was too big for her to grasp, so she didn't manifest anything. It was kind of like what would happen if someone suggested marriage on the first date. When Nan took the course again and focused on $10,000, she manifested a big check and new job that equated to more than $10,000. She has experience now, so she can go for bigger and bigger numbers. Start with $10,000 as your intention and master the process, then you can start upping your game with bigger and bigger amounts.

## 2. Identify Your Abundance Feelings

In order to manifest your desire, you have to feel now like you're going to feel when you have your intention. In other words, if having more money will make you feel peaceful, you can't attract more money by being stressed out. It simply doesn't work that way. You can't be stressed out over a list of manifesting tools you think you should be doing while trying to manifest money that will make you feel at peace. I have found this to be one of the hardest concepts for people to put into practice. It was also one of the biggest lessons I learned and it had the biggest impact on my success. Getting in touch with how you're going to *feel* when you have $10,000, and experiencing those feelings often and now, is very important.

How are you going to feel when you've manifested $10,000? Write down your answer. How many feelings should you write down? No more than three. Remember that when it comes to manifesting, *less* equals more success. By choosing one to three feelings that describe how you're going to feel when you have $10,000, that narrows your focus to the most important feeling or feelings. Coming up with a list of 20 ways you're going to feel when you manifest $10,000 dilutes the actual feelings. You really only need one feeling, but you can list up to three. The last time I went through the process I realized that the feeling I would have would be *freedom* or *feeling free*. *Feeling free* was the only thing I needed to focus on to experience success. I was not only successful at manifesting my $10,000, but many more opportunities opened up for greater amounts of freedom – and money – to flow into my life.

Before moving on, make sure that the feeling or feelings you've written down are actually feelings. Many people get off track right here, because they start focusing on a feeling that's not a feeling. Here are some common feelings:

- Free
- Peaceful
- Calm
- Excited
- Accomplished
- Joyful
- Happy

An example of something that's not a feeling is, "I would have what I need." That is not a feeling. If you came up with a feeling statement like that, ask yourself, "What will I feel like when I have what I need?" Keep drilling down until you get to an actual feeling.

Once you've identified how you're going to feel when you have manifested $10,000, make a list of ten ways you can activate those feelings. Some of them might require a financial investment, but the majority most likely won't. If you find they all do, keep adding to your list of ways, then identify the ones you can do daily or weekly, and put them on your calendar. I suggest setting an alarm on your phone to remind you to activate your feelings, until it becomes habit to activate them every day.

This part can sometimes be tricky. A client of mine, Lindsey, did this assignment and wrote down *confidence* as her feeling. As I was explaining the next part of the assignment (coming up below), I felt that something was off with her. When I asked her if confident was really how she was going to feel when she was holding $10,000, she said, "My thinking is that it's easier to manifest what I want when I feel confident as I am. What I want is freedom. Freedom is the ultimate goal, but right this second it's more difficult to think up ten things to help me feel free, because, if I'm totally honest, I feel rather trapped right now."

What Lindsey said is exactly what is going to keep her from manifesting $10,000. You have to feel now like you are going to feel when you have $10,000 in your hand. It's so easy to think, "It will be easier to manifest if I do (fill in the blank)," especially when it seems easier than doing what feels hard, like finding a way to feel free when you are currently feeling trapped.

Manifesting is easy, but it requires a lot of hard work – not hard work in the traditional sense, but the hard work of changing who you are and what you're experiencing. Who you are now is the reason you have manifested whatever you have now. In order to manifest something different, you have to become a different version of yourself.

I wish I could say it's going to be so easy, but the truth is that it's often hard. It's easy to write down a list of feelings and not *really* think about the depth needed for the manifesting to happen. It's easy to write down only five ways, instead of ten, to activate that feeling, but it's not going to get you what you desire. Doing the hard work of expanding your mind and your being is what makes the rest of it easy. Once you understand this, manifesting is easy, but there's a lot of hard work that goes into what makes manifesting easy. I've spent lots of time doing the hard work, and the conclusion I have come to is that it's much easier to do the hard work up front to make manifesting easier, as opposed to staying the same and experiencing the same struggle every day. It is a choice you are going to have to make as well.

Lindsey said, "It's hard to think of ways to feel free right now." That's exactly why it's important that she figures out how to experience freedom right now. It's important that you do it, too. When you do, in addition to getting more of what you focus on, you get more of what you're experiencing. If you're experiencing feeling trapped most of the time, you are creating more of that.

When I went through the Manifest 10K process the first time, I clarified that *free* was the feeling I was going to feel when I had an additional $10,000. I also came up with a list of ways I could activate feeling free, because I didn't feel free at that time. One of the simplest ways I came up with was to watch a *Friends* episode in the afternoon. To me, that felt like freedom because it reminded me of being in college when I felt like I had more time freedom, so I could watch one of my favorite shows in the middle of the afternoon. Making a point to stop working and watch *Friends* every day made me feel free, and that opened the door to manifesting $10,000.

Everyone is unique. What makes you feel free, or any other feeling, isn't going to be the same as what activates feeling free in me. Your list has to be uniquely you and tailored to your specific feeling.

Investing the time now to identify your abundance feelings and add the activation of them into your routine will exponentially increase your success manifesting $10,000.

### 3. Focus on What You Want

One of the biggest mistakes I see people make is that when they start the process of manifesting money they're at a place where they have been having some sort of lack mindset going on. In other words, they decided to start manifesting money because there hasn't been enough. Jumping into some of the common manifesting techniques like visualizing or creating a vision board, before you've shifted your focus, can lead to disappointment.

This is why the third phase of the Manifest 10K process is all about focusing on money. Not manifesting it, just getting your brain used to seeing more of it. We use several fun exercises that put the focus on money without the attachment of manifesting it. When you start your money manifesting, take one to ten days to increase your focus on money so that your awareness of it heightens. Turn noticing money into a game as much as possible, so that you're having fun while increasing your focus. One way you can do this is to engage in a money scavenger hunt. Start by setting the intention of finding a penny. Once you find a penny, start finding a nickel. (I'm saying "finding" intentionally; you could "look" forever but your actual intention is to "find.") Continue "upping" the amount as you find the next thing on your list. They might sound silly, but games like this actually shift your focus in a way that *feels* fun and not forced, so they are setting the stage for your success. Making it a game keeps it light and fun so that when you take manifesting to the next level your brain is open to light and fun, which are two states of being that increase the speed and ease of manifesting.

This creates very fertile ground to then start doing manifesting exercises. In the same way a farmer wants to make sure the ground is ready to plant seeds, you want to make sure that you have fertile ground in which to plant your manifesting seeds. The better the soil, the better the growth – in this case, the more money will show up. Many people jump right in and start planting seeds before they are ready.

One of the ways we create even more fertile ground in the Manifest 10K course is by having a Facebook group. When you're involved with a large number of people who are all cultivating the same energy with their focus, it adds to the fertility of your intentions. With synergy, people focusing together create more for each person than they would create by acting alone. Well, imagine being in a space where hundreds of people are focusing on manifesting $10,000 and are sharing all their evidence. The energy builds, so it takes less effort, in terms of manifesting activities, to attract $10,000. Is there a friend you could invite on your manifesting journey with you, to take advantage of this synergistic effect?

## 4. Allow Money into Your Life

After you have created very fertile ground for planting your intentions, the next step is to allow them to grow. The farmer doesn't plant seeds one day and go out and pull them out of the ground the next day to see if they're growing. He trusts that once he's planted them, all he has to do is care for them and they will grow. His manifesting in that way is easier for him than it may be for you at this point, because he has planted crops before and seen them grow. Even if it is his first time, he knows other farmers who have planted their crops and the crops have grown, so he can trust that it's going to happen.

How can you practice allowing? One way is to accept all that you receive. Whether it's receiving a compliment, a free drink, or $10,000, the act of allowing starts with being able to receive. You can't deflect a compliment and allow more money into your life. You're either someone who receives or you're not.

You met Aaron in Chapter 3. Here's what he had to say about learning to receive: "I really enjoyed the part of the program where we were told to accept whatever is offered to us. I grew up being told to say, 'No, thank you,' because my parents thought it was polite and they didn't want to take away from someone else. However, I realized several years ago that not accepting a gift from someone not only deprives me of goodness, it also takes away the goodness the giver receives from giving. This part of the program really helped to cement that new way of thinking into my life, because – out of habit – I still would say, 'No, thank you' sometimes."

When you're manifesting $10,000 for the first time, it can be harder to trust. Maybe you don't have a lot of friends who have manifested $10,000 who you can borrow that trust from. This is why it's built into the Manifest 10K course to practice allowing. It puts the focus on allowing and receiving instead of on anxiously watching for seeds to sprout.

One way you can practice this is to visualize yourself as a football receiver. This might sound weird, but bear with me. No football receiver intentionally deflects the pass his quarterback throws. However, I often see manifestors deflect what the Universe sends. So, imagine yourself as the receiver and picture yourself catching a bunch of money that the Universe is throwing at you. Coming at the receiving aspect in a bunch of fun ways makes it easier to open up and receive all that you are asking for. If you are not going to receive it, what is the point in asking for it?

Allowing takes practice. One of the ways to practice is to keep your focus on your feelings. Another is to practice being who you will be when you have $10,000. For example, if you are then going to give some money away, do some of that now, so you can be in touch with that feeling. Also, you can appreciate all the money you already have. After you have planted your seeds, and you've done whatever you choose to do to practice allowing, make sure you refrain from pulling your seeds out to see if they have grown. In other words, don't sit around saying, "I don't see any money manifesting." Instead, be patient and allow money to start flowing in.

The most important thing is to remember that allowing takes practice. If you aren't already a good receiver, you're going to have to practice until receiving becomes second nature. You can definitely do it, and it will greatly increase your success with manifesting.

## 5. Create Your New Money Beliefs

Earlier in the book, I mentioned that many people are not successful at manifesting more money because they're focused on trying to fix limiting beliefs. Their process goes something like this: identify a limiting belief and try to replace it with the opposite belief. The problem with this method is that you're trying to override the old belief. With a lot of energy, effort, and diligence that is totally possible. And, yes, there are some great techniques for releasing and shifting limiting beliefs to make that process easier. However, the residue of the old beliefs will remain.

I'm not sure what prompted our conversation, but when I was 15 years old and in the car with my dad, he told me that his salary amount was in the top 1% in the U.S. He went on to say how lucky he was and how lucky we were as a family. I remember listening and being freaked out. We didn't live in a bad neighborhood, but we definitely were not "rich" in the way I thought of rich people being. We didn't live in the best part of the city, and my dad had worked *so* hard to get to that place. When I was younger, he'd worked 80 hours a week. By the time I was 15, he probably worked 50 to 60 hours a week. On top of that, my dad told me he believed he'd gotten lucky seven times in his career, meaning he'd been in the right place at the right time seven times.

The way my 15-year-old brain processed that was to think that I would never have enough money. I'm guessing he was making $100,000 a year at the time. I thought that if we were in the top 1% (the U.S. has a big spread, by the way) and had to work so hard to get there *and* he'd gotten lucky, there was *no way* I was ever going to be able to get to that level of income. Being in the right place at the right time is hardly plannable, and I didn't want to work 60-plus hours a week.

You can imagine the limiting beliefs that came out of that conversation! *I have to work hard to make a lot of money. I have to get lucky to make a lot of money. There is no way for me to make a lot of money.* I spent many years trying to *fix* those beliefs. I would energetically shift them and replace them with something new, yet that didn't seem to be working. That's because every time I thought it wasn't working, I would go back and try and fix some version of those beliefs and thus take on a new, related belief.

The problem was that every new belief that was created as an antidote to one of those limiting beliefs still carried enough residue from the limiting belief that it was still limiting. I was trying to fix the current version of myself, a version that did not have the money I wanted, instead of stepping into the version of myself that did have the money I desired.

Finally, I realized I had a choice about what I believed – I could choose my beliefs, and they did not have to be created as a way to fix any of the other beliefs. Once I just decided what I wanted my money beliefs to be and started focusing on those instead of trying to "correct" the old limiting beliefs, things started to shift very quickly. In part, that was because I had been creating fertile ground for new thoughts by focusing on money and the feelings I wanted to have. I also had clarity about what I wanted.

I created my beliefs on a blank page, instead of editing an old version of myself to try to take the story where I wanted it to go. I simply wrote down my new beliefs as I wanted them to be – as I wanted myself to be – without looking at what my beliefs currently were. When I created the beliefs from that new place of choosing the beliefs I wanted, they were much better for me and much stronger – and they naturally replaced the old limiting beliefs. Those old beliefs never came up again. Many of the new beliefs I created were ones I had tried for years to get to take hold. They just hadn't been able to when they were the antidote. When I chose them from the blank space, they became the driving force behind manifesting money easily and quickly.

That is why – about one month into the Manifest 10K process – it's good to create the money beliefs you desire. By this time, you're choosing the beliefs you want to have about money because you have experienced success manifesting, you have seen others manifest money, you have read lots of stories about money manifesting in magical ways, you have kept your focus on money, you're clear about what you truly desire, and you're activating your abundance feelings on a regular basis. Talk about fertile ground! You're at the perfect place to choose your money beliefs and allow them to start guiding your money life.

It is important to choose the money beliefs that you genuinely want to guide your journey. It's even more important to choose them at the right time, so they have the right energy and momentum behind them. I suggest doing this after you've spent about a month on the previous five phases. Once you've created momentum and a shift in your perspective, sit down and choose what you want to believe about money. You will be amazed at how the beliefs created in this manner will take hold and start guiding the manifestation of money quickly and easily.

## 6. Create Your New Money Persona

When you have your new beliefs locked in, take it even further and create a money persona. Many people talk about creating a new money story, and while I am all about creating a new story, I believe that starts with a strong character, which is your money persona. This is the next phase of the Manifest 10K process.

Your money persona is a characterization of who you desire to be in terms of money. Your money persona encompasses your goals, thoughts, beliefs, intentions, and feelings. It is basically a representation of everything you think and feel about money, and that is in keeping with your goals and intentions. It's the complete person that you are stepping into.

Why is it important to create a money persona? So that when you're interacting with the world you can check in with your money persona to see what he or she would do.

When you build a complete character file of who you desire to become regarding money, you have a reference point for how you think and feel about this issue and – most importantly – how you want to make decisions. When you have something to reference, you know the answer more quickly, because you're not guessing, you're becoming.

We talked earlier about how important *beingness* is to manifesting more money, and how people who only do manifesting activities but don't step into the *beingness* are less successful at manifesting more money. Having a defined money persona allows you to more fully step into the *beingness* quickly and easily, which, in turn, makes manifesting money quick and easy.

In order to create your money persona, think about creating a character for a TV show. Start with what your goals are. For this part, think beyond the $10,000 and ask yourself what your long-term financial goals are. What do you really want your life to look like? Then think about how that person – the version of you that lives that life – thinks about money, feels about money, and what do they do with their money? How do they behave when it comes to their money? Write all of this down so that you can reference it anytime you need it.

You could let the answers come right now, but I recommend not doing this exercise now if you haven't done the steps above. Waiting to do this until after you've built momentum by completing the other phases of the process first can bring you more success.

I recently moved to The Enchanted Palace, which is what I call my home – my apartment in a high-rise, high in the sky above Denver. When I'm up here and looking down, I can see so many things that I'd had no idea existed. For example, I had no idea how many rooftop pools, patios, and gardens there are in the city. Up high, I'm looking down on them, so I can see them. If you create your money persona at the beginning of the manifesting process, that's like creating it while being on the ground floor. You have not yet come to know that so much more is possible for you. However, if you build up momentum first, before you create your money persona, that's like riding the elevator up to my floor. From here, you can look around and get a different perspective. You can see so much more, and you can create a money persona that serves you better. The better your money persona is with money, the easier money will manifest when you begin stepping into that persona.

## 7. Integrate Your Money Persona into Your Life

After you have created your money persona, the next phase is to integrate your money persona's life into your life. Shifting your physical reality to reflect that of your money persona's is a shortcut to *becoming* your money persona. When you start moving pieces of your physical life around to mirror the life your money persona is living, things start to manifest faster. Money shows up even more easily and quickly.

Once you've created your money persona, think about your money persona's home and how it looks, the car your money persona drives, the places your money persona goes. Most people, at this point, especially if they start thinking about this before going through the rest of the phases, start experiencing resistance and thinking they don't have the money to do these things.

But experiencing your physical reality as your money persona would experience it doesn't have to take a lot of money.

There are lots of ways to experience the life of your money persona now. For example, if they live in a different neighborhood, you can go have coffee in that neighborhood, or park your car there and walk around as if you live there. You can buy one or two things at the food store you would be shopping at. If your money persona indulges in amazing dinners at fancy restaurants, go have a drink at the bar so you know what it feels like to be in the middle of the experience. You can research and start planning that trip your money persona would be booking tickets for. You will see so many possibilities when you create your money persona after you have gone through the other phases.

Most people miss this step. You can definitely manifest by simply visualizing how things are going to go, but the process speeds up when your physical reality starts to match that of your money persona. When you know and feel the physical experience, it's easier to manifest. Also, it's like attracts like. The more money persona experiences you have now, the more will naturally be manifested into your life. When you look around your life, you need to see that your life is changing, because that triggers your brain to start expecting different experiences. Because your brain creates your current reality based on your memories, making changes in your physical reality clues your brain in that you're creating a new reality. If nothing in your physical experience changes, your brain will try to recreate the same experience you've been having. It's the way your brain works. By changing your physical reality, you're able to interrupt your brain's process of recreating the same experiences over and over again.

## 8. Step Into the Experience

The final semester of the Manifest 10K course is all about experiencing fully being the version of yourself who not only has $10,000, but who has more than enough money. Throughout the previous seven phases, you built momentum and gained insight into what it feels like to have the money you desire, and you've experienced how it can come into your life. During this last phase, you step into the future and use all of those experiences to help you tap into the feeling of having *more than enough* money on a daily basis. We do this by scripting.

Scripting is a process of writing down an experience you want to have as if it has already happened. Scripting every day about an amazing experience you want to have with money, as if it has already happened, activates your *beingness* of having money on a consistent basis. Doing this after you've gone through all the other phases really allows you to open up and see the possibility of having more than enough money. Being open to that allows you to tap into the experience so you can script it in more detail and really feel like you are in the experience.

Scripting involves writing down the experience you desire *as if it has already happened*. When you do that, you create pathways in your brain that support that experience. You also, as you write, literally experience what you want, so you're creating a memory of what it feels like, which makes the experience much more likely to repeat in reality. You are also solely focused on what you want, and that momentum carries you forward.

### The Breakdown of the Phases

I consider each of the 30-day segments of the 90-day Manifest 10K process to be a *trimester*. Here's how the trimesters break down:

**Trimester 1 – Days 1-30:**

1. Get clear about what you want
2. Identify your abundance feelings
3. Focus on what you want
4. Allow money into your life

**Trimester 2 – Days 31-60:**

1. Create your new money beliefs
2. Create your new money persona
3. Integrate your new money persona into your life

**Trimester 3 – Days 61-90:**

1. Step into the Experience

**All Three Semesters:**

Amp up your belief in what is possible

Celebrate early and often

## Amp Up Your Belief in What is Possible

Amping up your belief is included in every trimester. You'll do some of that throughout the entire 90-day process. In order to amp up your belief and open your possibility channels, read one story a day for the first 30 days about magical ways money has manifested into people's lives. Then, for trimesters two and three, read at least one story a week. Remember that you can use the ones in this book to get you started.

In an earlier chapter, I talked about the ways people think money manifests. The reason they think the way they do is that their brains cannot come up with other ways, because they don't know other ways. You have started the process of opening up those possibility channels by reading the stories in this book of people who have manifested money.

I share those stories because opening those channels is a key part of the manifesting process. It's so important that I built it into the Manifest 10K program. I start every assignment by telling a possibility-opening story. Most of them are my personal stories about shifting my focus toward abundance and how money started to show up in ways that were beyond my imagination. I share them because when you read them and hear them, your thoughts about what's possible regarding how many ways money can manifest in your life are expanded.

After you hear or read enough of those stories, you naturally start letting go of needing to know the "how." Letting go of the "how" is possibly the greatest barrier deliberate creators come up against. Your brain naturally thinks it has to figure out how the money manifestation is going to happen in order for it to happen. Because it doesn't know all the magical ways the Universe can deliver, it starts to fixate on one of the ways it thinks it can happen. As we have discussed, when you're *trying to figure out the how*, you're not actually leveraging the power of the Law of Attraction. However, when you flood your consciousness with amazing stories of money just showing up, your brain naturally starts to let go of needing to know the *how* in advance. When you let go, you can truly allow in all the abundance you desire.

You have started the process of opening up your possibility channels by reading the stories in this book. To keep that up, engage with more stories of money showing up. You can reread the stories in this book, and GoodVibeBlog.com has tons of stories on it about money showing up. You can also do a search about this topic on the Internet. However you find the stories, start your process with reading them, because they are the key to opening up your possibility channels. They help you let go of the "how," and that will lead to manifesting $10,000 quickly and easily.

## Celebrate Early and Often

Celebrating along the way is not only going to help you manifest quicker and easier, it is going to make the journey much more fun. This is part of how you train your brain to start seeing what you would like to see more of when it comes to money. Celebrate finding pennies on the ground. Yes, that might sound silly because it is just a penny. However, if you see money as money and you start celebrating every time more of it shows up in your life, it is going to show up more in your life.

Remember, like attracts like and you will always get more of what you focus on. I once read an article about a runner who found hundreds of dollars on the ground while he was running each year. His friend, who also ran, didn't find any money when he was running. What was the difference? One of them was looking and expecting to find money, and the other was not looking. The more you look for all the ways more money is showing up in your life and acknowledge it, the more money is going to show up in your life.

Celebration turns your attention to what you want to experience more of. To make celebrating really powerful and super-charge your attraction, keep track of both how money is coming into your life and how evidence is showing up around you. For example, last year, at the last minute, I was offered a free place to stay in Hawaii for two weeks. I posted that on Facebook, and my friend told me she counted that as evidence for herself, because she was wanting to manifest a free place to stay in Hawaii. The tendency can be to assume that when someone else gets what you want, that means you did something wrong. But what if it actually means that what you desire is getting closer to you? If you celebrate that as evidence of what you want being on its way, then what you desire will show up much more quickly.

Celebrating makes the journey more fun, and once you learn to enjoy the journey everything else becomes easier. Do you remember Amanda, from a previous chapter? Here's her advice to someone who's trying to manifest money: "Truly enjoy the journey – that will be the most rewarding thing you'll ever do." Celebrating as often as possible makes it easy to enjoy the journey. The more you celebrate, the more you will find to celebrate.

## Chapter 6

# Set Yourself up to Manifest $10,000

*a*re you imagining having $10,000 in your hand? Are you visualizing what it will feel like to board the plane and head to the beach? Can you see the bank statement showing lots of money in savings? When you think about your life in 90 days, how do you feel? In the previous chapter I gave you the phases to successfully manifest $10,000 in the next 90 days. Now I'll share with you the ways to ensure that you stay on course.

One of the things I see that detours people from manifesting $10,000 in 90 days is that they don't allow themselves the full 90 days. They start freaking out at day four or day 14 because "nothing is happening." Then they decide that "something is wrong" and go right back down the path we talked about earlier: they start focusing on what is wrong, so they start finding evidence that something is wrong. They shift their focus, and because they start seeing things as "not working," they stop doing the real work. They find lots of evidence that what they're doing isn't working.

The key is to keep going in the direction of "it's happening." Donna, who has experienced success in the Manifest 10K course, gives this advice to people who want to manifest money: "Do the work! Most of the exercises are fun and feel good, so you're losing nothing by doing them, and the added benefit is that cool stuff happens, money comes in, freebies appear, your money goes further than you expect, and your attitude changes." People who do the Manifest 10K process experience success. Those who start strong but stop in the middle, who never make it to the end, don't experience much success. The key to success with this process is doing all of it. If you can figure out how to finish, you will experience success.

What gets in the way of people finishing?

The first reason people don't finish is that they don't commit to going all into the process and finishing it. Making the commitment up front to stick with it for 90 days greatly increases your chances of success.

The process takes practice to make it habit. Remember that you're changing who you are, including how your brain operates. How long has it been operating the way it's currently operating? It's not going to magically change overnight, and you're not going to just become the person, the version of yourself, who has an additional $10,000 overnight. That's why it's important to commit to doing the whole process for the next 90 days, and not freak out when you think it's not working.

How do you do that?

First, you commit 20 minutes a day to the process right now. If you're all in, stop reading and put 20 minutes a day into your schedule for the next 90 days. Simply putting the time in your calendar increases your chances of success by 50%.

You know it's a likely probability that you will hit a point when you'll think, "This isn't working" – so how do you get through that? First, because you know it is likely to happen, you're more likely to get through it. Second, you stay committed to doing the process for 20 minutes every day, no matter what. The third thing that you can do is pre-plan what you are going to do. In the previous chapter, I gave you the timeline of what to focus on and when during the 90 days. Adding those to your calendar now makes it more likely that you will succeed, because you will not have to think about what to do next at any point. The fourth way to increase your chances of success is to focus on manifesting $10,000 over the next 90 days, rather than trying to also manifest other things or amounts over different time spans. Stephen Covey says, "Begin with the end in mind," and that is the fifth way to ensure you will be successful. The sixth is to do everything presented in this book. The seventh thing is to enlist support.

**Commit to Success**

Did you put the 20 minutes a day on your calendar? If you haven't yet, go ahead and do it now. Seriously, this is step one to being as successful as possible in manifesting

$10,000 in the next 90 days. Putting that 20 minutes in your calendar can mean the difference between manifesting $10,000 instead of $0.

Is putting it on your calendar a strong enough commitment to yourself? Or is there something else you need to also do, like write out your commitment to yourself, or tell someone who will help keep you accountable? Take a moment to think about times when you have been successful in the past; it can be about manifesting or about something else. Now think about some times when you didn't stick with something or were not as successful as you wanted to be. In the instances where you experienced success, how did you make the commitment to be successful? In the instances where you were not successful, what was missing in terms of commitment? Use all of those examples from your own life to determine how you're going to commit to your success. Take the time, right now, before you go on reading. Write down what you came up with.

How can you use the examples of times you did and did not experience success to not only ensure you are committed right now, but to make sure you stay committed when the going gets tough? Growing is awesome, but it is not always easy. I would be lying to you if I said this process was going to be a breeze and all sunshine and roses – because it's not. Changing is challenging for a variety of reasons. When you start changing your thought patterns, your brain can literally go through a detox process. That isn't fun. It usually involves a lot of crying or experiencing emotions that don't make sense. It gets better if you stay committed and keep going, but when you are in it, it's not fun and, honestly, your brain will tell you it's a reason to quit.

Can you look back and see a time when you quit in the process of change or manifesting and see that you might have been experiencing brain detox? It can get frustrating when you have to keep reminding yourself of things like "focus on what I want" when your habit has been to focus on things you don't want. If you don't see what you consider good enough results immediately, it can be challenging to keep going.

You are going to change during this process. That is inevitable because, in order to become the person who has 10,000 additional dollars, you have to change. Sometimes, that feels scary. It can feel like you don't know yourself anymore. I know what it feels like when I'm going through a big change. It feels like things are falling apart. Have you ever felt like that when you were in the midst of growing and changing? Did you stop or did you keep going? It really does get better, but in order for it to get better, you have to sit in the uncomfortableness for a while. If I could make it so that you didn't experience discomfort while you were going through the process, I would, but I can't, because it is all part of the process.

The key to getting through it, really, is to keep going. Based on your past successes, how can you ensure that you will keep going, even when it doesn't feel good? How can you make the commitment to yourself, right now, to keep going, even when it gets hard? Take a minute to think about that and to brainstorm how to ensure that you will stick with the process for 90 days.

As you continue on, keep in mind how you've ensured success in the past. There are clues in there that will help you be as successful as possible when it comes to manifesting $10,000 in the next 90 days.

Most people add doing the Manifest 10K process to their "list," but the people who experience the most success in the program make the Manifest 10K process their entire list. What does that mean? It means that when they commit 90 days to manifesting $10,000, they put all their other manifesting techniques on hold so they can focus on one thing: manifesting $10,000. That doesn't mean they spend hours and hours on it. It means they invest their 20 minutes a day wholeheartedly. In most cases, they invest less time in "manifesting" than they did before, when they were trying to complete their manifesting "list" everyday. Because they don't feel overwhelmed and guilty over not getting everything on a big list done, they have more energy available to feel good, which is how they need to feel now if they're going to manifest $10,000 – because it's how they'll feel when they have succeeded.

Here are the reasons why you're more likely to manifest if you're focusing on just one thing. If you've been working on manifesting something for a while, letting go while you focus on something else will give that thing room to manifest. The second reason is that you'll be more successful if you're focusing on only one thing, because that focus allows you to step more into the being instead of staying in the doing. It also allows you to become familiar with the process of manifesting in a step-by-step way, which allows you to level up your manifesting skills and take the opportunity to become a master manifestor. By focusing on manifesting $10,000, you internalize the process for manifesting more quickly and easily. Once you've learned it with $10,000, you can repeat it with anything. The best part is that you will know how to do it. You will know what you need to focus on in order to manifest the big things you want, and you'll know which of those other manifesting techniques on your "list" you can just let go of.

Once you commit to doing the process, make a commitment to getting really clear about what you want and focusing only on that desire. This will take practice if you realized while reading this book that you've been focusing on things you don't desire more of, like debt. The clarity and focus phases can be tricky if you rush through them. Allow yourself the time allocated (in the trimester phases and in your 20 minutes a day, every day) to first get crystal clear on what it is you want your $10,000 for, and then to check your focus and make sure it's 100% pointed toward what you desire. Those two things are keys to experiencing manifesting success.

Another thing I see people do that keeps them from being successful when they read a book about manifesting is picking out bits and pieces of the process and only doing those. You may or may not have success doing that. You are much more likely, however, to have success if you follow the entire, proven system.

If something has been proven to work for more than several people, it's likely that it will work for you, too. It will feel new and foreign, but that's because it's new to you. This process has been used hundreds of times and has generated hundreds of thousands of dollars for those who have used it. If you pick and choose only pieces of the process to add to your current manifesting routine, you are inventing a new process – one that has not yet been proven.

When you thought back on the times you experienced the most success in your life, did you realize that you had a clear vision of the outcome when you started the process? As I mentioned before, Stephen Covey says, "Start with the end in mind." You know you want to have an additional $10,000 in 90 days. In order to add depth to that desire, I suggest that you write out your experience as if it is 90 days from now and you have already manifested your $10,000. Tap into how it's going to feel and what your experiences were along the way. Put yourself 90 days from now and write out the experience you had.

You just had your calendar open, so you know what the date is 90 days from now. Take out a piece of paper or open up a file on your computer and date it 90 days from now. Put yourself in the middle of that day, knowing that you've manifested $10,000. Write about how happy you are that you committed yourself to the 90 days in order to make this happen. Write about how it feels to have $10,000. Write about how much you appreciate yourself and the money. Write about what you're going to do with the money and how that feels. Write about how you committed and stuck with it and how proud you are of yourself.

Writing out your success sets the GPS point that you're headed towards. It gets your brain involved in the process. Because your brain knows where you're going, it will help to keep you on track. Writing out that day also makes it less likely that you'll wander off course. If this type of exercise is new to you, I'll give you the formula I give people who are starting Manifest 10K so they can guide themselves:

I just finished the Manifest 10K course. It was so _____. I learned so much. I was surprised that _____. I was excited that _____. I can't believe _____.

Writing out the experience you're going to have, as if it's already happened, adds to the chances of your success. This is an introduction to the technique of scripting. You will go more in depth with using scripting after all the other phases, toward the end of the process. However, here at the beginning of the process, it's important to do this one script up front, so that you set your GPS to where you're going to be 90 days from now.

What else did you think of when you remembered your greatest successes? Did you have support? Maybe a parent or friend who cheered you on? Enlisting a team of cheerleaders will greatly increase your success in following the Manifest 10K process because it's more fun to have someone to celebrate with. One way to create support is to get a bunch of friends together to do the process with. That way you can cheer each other on. Can you think of two friends who would like to join you on the journey to manifesting $10,000?

Support is an important part of the Manifest 10K process. One of the things that makes the Manifest 10K program so successful is the built-in support system. There are hundreds of people in all different stages of the process in the program's Facebook group. The participants encourage each other and celebrate together. They hold space for one another's successes. They share their progress and visit the group whenever they need encouragement or a possibility jolt. If you commit to manifesting $10,000 in the next 90 days, I highly recommend that you find or create a support system that will be there for you during the process.

The amount of support you receive while growing and changing has a direct effect on how quickly and easily the change will occur. Surrounding yourself with people who understand where you are and who cheer you on can make all the difference. Many people who come to the Manifest 10K program don't feel like they have any other place to share their manifesting process and progress. They often feel like their family and friends will judge them or think they are weird. So finding support for the Manifest 10K process – finding a manifesting family for this journey – is crucial to your success in manifesting $10,000 in the next 90 days.

The other type of support that will increase your probability of success is having a coach. We discussed that it's going to feel at times like things are falling apart and don't feel good. In those moments, the thing that is most likely to keep you moving forward is someone who can remind you that "this is all part of the process" and to keep going when the going gets tough. Just having someone reminding you to keep moving forward can make the difference between success and failure. Have you ever experienced that in your life? If you got a group of friends together, you could also hold each other accountable.

*Chapter 7*

# 90 Days from Now

*C*an you feel the $10,000 in your hands, taste the mai tai, hear the song blasting in your paid-off car, see the big number in your savings account, or smell the salt of the ocean yet? You have everything you need to make all of those, and more, a reality.

You can do this! You can not only manifest $10,000 in 90 days, but also develop a better relationship with money and learn the foundation of manifesting anything your heart desires. You can use this book and go through all the steps and be successful. However, if you are sitting there thinking, "I wish someone would just tell me what to do every day and provide a place where I can show up and share my successes along the way and cheer others on while they are cheering me on"… wish granted. Simply go to Manifest10K.com and register for the Manifest 10K course.

Are you wondering how much it costs? Here's the beauty: the course is pay-after-you-manifest. That means you can get started now for $1, which is a tribute to your future manifestations, and simply pay a portion of whatever you manifest on your journey. I created the course just for you!

Cheers to all of your money manifesting success!

# About the Author

Cassie Parks loves the ocean, dancing for no reason, and celebrating with champagne, but what she loves most of all is living a life a she loves. She is a bestselling author, international speaker, and coach whose passion is leading others to live the life they have been dreaming about.

Cassie retired at 32 by combining her love for real estate and the Law of Attraction to create financial independence. She believes you can create anything you desire, even that dream you've been too afraid to admit to having.

Cassie is the host of the popular *Manifest it Now* podcast and the creator of the Manifest 10K course, which has helped hundreds of people develop better relationships with money and manifest more money into their lives. Her one-of-a-kind Enchanted Future workshop allows people to discover that they can be their own magic wand and create a life full of dreams come true.

When Cassie isn't writing, speaking, or coaching you can find her traveling the world, sitting on her Denver balcony soaking up the mountain view, or enjoying the company of her friends and family.

Cassie's life motto is: You are worthy of living the best story you can tell.

# Thank You

I am so excited to get you on the path to manifesting $10,000 that I'll even make it fun and easy.

When you register for the Manifest 10K program, you'll get:

1. The option to pay $1 now and the rest after you manifest more money, so that you can get started right away.
2. Access to the Facebook group, aka the hottest money manifesting party, so that you can share your successes and benefit from the group's momentum.

3. Course emails, delivered to your inbox, so that you know exactly what to do each day.

4. Access to over 30 hours of recordings on money manifesting, so that you have everything you need to manifest $10,000 in the next 90 days.

Simply go to Manifest10K.com to get started!

# The Morgan James
## Speakers Group

Morgan James makes all of our titles available
through the Library for All Charity Organizations.

www.LibraryForAll.org

9 781683 501961